MW01616421

THE REVEAL™

rudy**ruettiger** & nikkos**zorbas**

about**rudy**

The man whose story of valor inspired millions in the acclaimed 1993 film *Rudy* continues to motivate audiences of all ages with his spirit of adversity over triumph.

In addition to speaking professionally, Rudy Ruettiger has co-authored several books and produced multimedia material including *The Reveal, Dream Big Never Quit* program.

Rudy founded and supports the RUDY FOUNDATION to help children around the world reach their full potential. *www.RudyInternational.com*

Dream big, never quit.

– DANIEL "RUDY" RUETTIGER

about**nikkos**

Renowned performance coach in the field of self-development, Nikkos Zorbas passionately helps people dream big and release their potential from within.

In addition to being the original concept creator of *The Reveal, Dream Big Never Quit* program, Nikkos is the producer of the international hit album, *The Law of Attraction*.

He believes that music moves the soul and by adding motivational lyrics, songs can truly rejuvenate and restore a person's well-being. Nikkos' website *www.NikkoSystem.com* reveals details about his speeches, seminars and coaching; *www.TheLawOfAttractionMusic.com* features his inspirational music.

Identify your desire and you will discover your power.

— Nikkos Zorbas

Acknowledgments

Authors: *Nikkos Zorbas, Rudy Ruettiger*

Publishers: *Rudy International, NikkoSystem, Inc.*

Editing: *Barbara McNichol, Linda Lou, and special thanks to Sophia Stavron*

Design: *Robert Schram, Bookends Publication Design*

ISBN 978-0-9820802-2-1

Printed in China

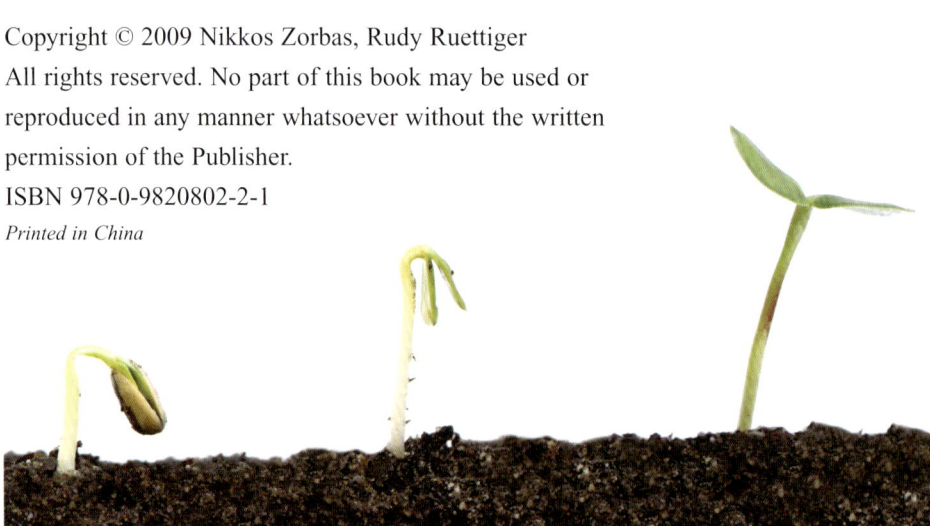

BUILD-A-BIG-DREAM
Journal

*E*VERYTHING BEGINS AS A THOUGHT. Like a seed, a thought needs a solid foundation, a supportive environment, and proper nourishment in order to flourish. Without these conditions, the thought withers and dies.

The journal you're holding started with a thought. We planted a seed to create a tool to complement *The Reveal, Dream Big Never Quit* program. Happily, that seed grew because we nourished the thought with our attention, energy, and focus. Now it's your turn to create a thought, plant the seed, and build a dream—a BIG dream!

– RUDY AND NIKKOS

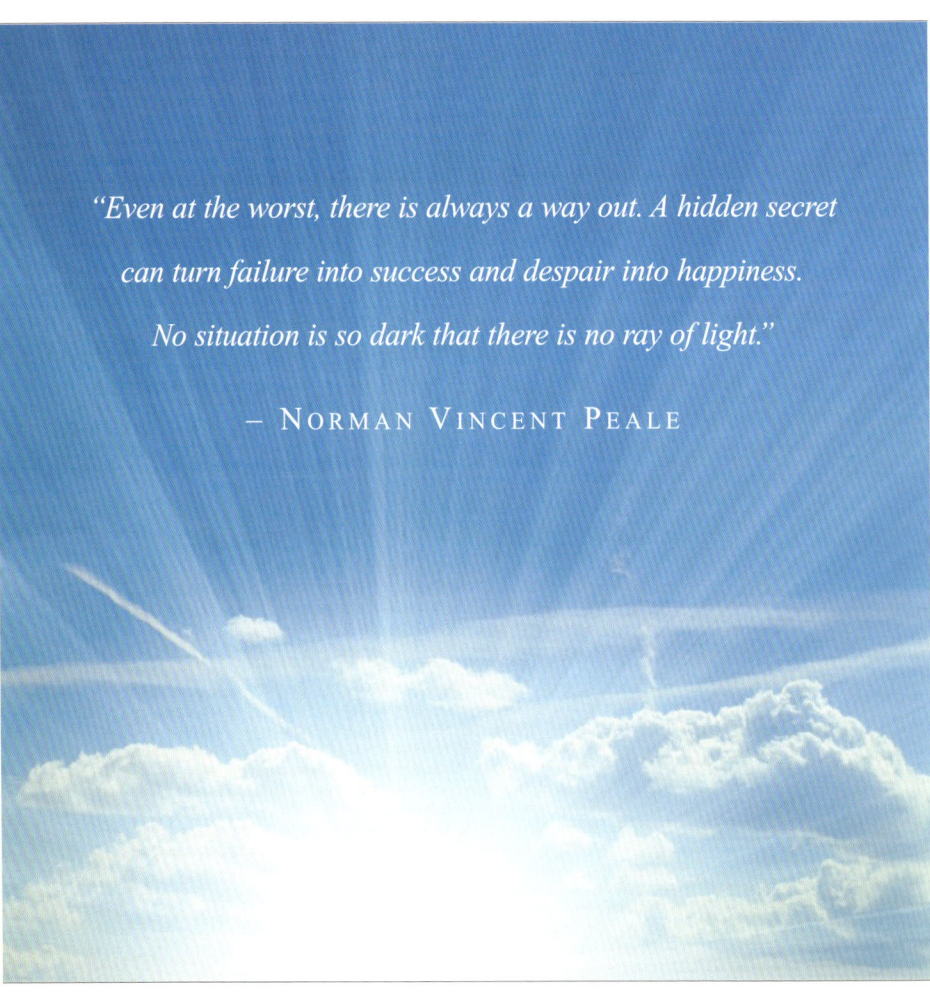

"Even at the worst, there is always a way out. A hidden secret can turn failure into success and despair into happiness. No situation is so dark that there is no ray of light."

— NORMAN VINCENT PEALE

BUILD-A-BIG-DREAM
Journal Contents

"My capabilities exceed my limitations."

– BRUCE LEE

PART 1

LET THE JOURNAL BEGIN

*T*HIS JOURNAL INCLUDES a series of exercises to help guide your thoughts and actions toward dreaming BIG and then manifesting your dreams.

Take each exercise to heart—don't rush through them—and feel free to write notes on the pages as you go. Additional journal entry pages have been provided at the end of the book.

You will never realize your success until you've given 100 percent of yourself to your dream. By holding this journal in your hands, you've already taken the first step.

> *"Go confidently in the directions of your dreams,*
> *live the life you've imagined."*
>
> – HENRY DAVID THOREAU

It all begins with a thought

Yes, every great creation begins with a dream. And every dream begins with a thought. Living the life you dream about is but a thought away.

What do you catch yourself thinking about? Does worry consume your thoughts? Or do your thoughts focus on building a wonderful future? Yesterday can't be changed; however, you can ruin the present by worrying about the future.

*Positive thoughts
attract positive experiences.*

Dream BIG notes

Visualize BIG dreams

Pretend you have a crystal ball in front of you. Visualize it as big and expansive.

In your mind's eye, gaze inside the crystal ball until you can see, smell, and taste your ideal life. Clearly envision as many details as you can. Notice how you feel as you're living your ideal life.

Now write down everything you saw in that crystal ball. Note every detail just as you envisioned.

Dream BIG notes

Identify your dream

Sometimes you can get so caught up in life's daily responsibilities and obligations, you feel like you've lost your ability to dream. Your answers to these questions will help REVEAL your true heart's desire.

1. What makes me happy?

2. What interests have I had since I was a child?

3. What have I truly enjoyed doing that I don't do anymore?

4. What is the one thing I enjoy doing so much that I'd do it for no pay?

5. What are some of my natural strengths?

6. If I could be known for one great thing in this world, what would it be?

7. If I knew I could not fail, what would I dare to become?

Create a dream vision board

*T*o help you clarify and attract your dreams, paste photos that represent your desires here.

"Change your thoughts and change your world."

— NORMAN VINCENT PEALE

PART 2

DREAMS, BELIEFS, AND THOUGHTS

Visualization

•

Believe, behave, and become

•

Imagine living your dream now

Visualization

You have big dreams inside you. The visualization exercise with the crystal ball helped you to see one of them—now you must believe it is possible to achieve.

The problem is, you may not fully believe in that dream.

Believe. It just might be the most powerful word ever.

Visualize yourself living your dreams until you believe them to be real.

Believe, behave, and become

To bring your dream into reality, you must *believe* in your ability to manifest that dream. You must *believe* in yourself—that is the most important thing.

Behave with great conviction towards your dream. When you do this, you will soon discover that your dream is beginning to *become* a reality.

How strongly do you *believe* in yourself? How strong is your conviction in achieving your dream?

Do you *believe* you can achieve your dream?

Believe you have it,
and you have it.

"Whether you think that you can,

or that you can't, you are usually right."

— HENRY FORD

Exercise: Imagine living your dream now

Did you know your mind cannot differentiate between a thought based on fact and a thought that's rooted in fantasy? Just by thinking about your dream, you bring it more toward reality; your mind cannot tell what's real and what's imagined. So in a sense, you've already lived your dream!

Imagine you're living your dream right this moment. How does that feel?

I keep my dream alive by keeping it in the forefront of my mind.

PART 3

THE LAW
OF ATTRACTION

The Law of Attraction is based on four principles

•

The Law of Attraction requires you to . . .

•

"I asked for a million and never got a penny"

•

Where attention goes, energy flows

•

Positive thoughts . . . pass them on!

The Law of Attraction is based on four principles:

- Like attracts like
- What goes around comes around (karma)
- What you put in, you get out
- You reap what you sow

If you've already imagined it, you've already started to attract it.

The greatest gift I can give my dream is my energy, attention, and action.

"I attract to myself whatever I focus my attention,

energy, and thoughts on . . . whether positive or negative,

wanted or unwanted."

The Law of Attraction requires you to

- Accept responsibility for everything in your life, good or bad
- Identify your desires and allow them to manifest
- Focus your mind, allowing only positive thoughts

The Law of Attraction is all about the vibrations you emanate. When you vibrate at a lower frequency, you feel negative emotions such as depression, anger, frustration, and fear. When you vibrate at a higher frequency, you feel positive emotions such as abundance, joy, passion, and appreciation.

You attract circumstances, people, and experiences that match your current vibration. You cannot attract positive forces to your life if your vibration is low. Therefore, it is important to continually be aware of your vibration and make a conscious effort to keep it raised.

I fill my mind with positive thoughts. I attract the things, people, and experiences I need to achieve my goal.

Exercise: Raise your vibration

You can raise your vibration anytime you want simply by pressing your "Reset" button, an imaginary button that instantly clears your mind.

Experiment with this right now—press your Reset button and think positive thoughts for a full 30 seconds. Do this whenever you feel your vibration is low.

You can go as far as your mind will let you.

Dream BIG notes

How did you feel when you pressed your Reset button?

Was it difficult to think positive thoughts for 30 seconds? Why?

What do you need to do differently next time?

How will you make this a habit?

"What you believe,

remember you can achieve."

– MARY KAY ASH

"I asked for a million and never got a penny"

Keep in mind that the Law of Attraction doesn't respond well to begging. You must identify your true heart's desire, be on purpose with it, and be willing to act on it.

Asking for a million dollars is too vague. Besides, a million dollars in itself is not really what you want; it's the feeling you'd get from what a million dollars could give you.

Dream BIG notes

What have you attracted in the past?

Name specific people, things and circumstances you know you've attracted in the past, whether you consciously wanted them or not.

Friends:

Finances:

Education:

Possessions:

Situations:

Where attention goes, energy flows

You attract whatever you predominantly think about. The question is, are you thinking about what you *don't* want instead of what you *do* want?

On the next page, write down in tiny letters the people, possessions, and circumstances you *don't* want. Then, in very large letters, write down each entry's opposite. For example, on the left side you may list *"high credit card balances"* and on the right, *"all my bills paid in full."* The contrast helps you to find clarity and focus your thoughts on what you want—that's what you'll attract into your life.

I will seek out
positive and supportive people.

Dream BIG notes

What I *don't* want

What I *do* want

Positive thoughts . . . pass them on!

When you pass on positive thoughts to others, you create a caring energy and great things happen. The best part is, the recipients of your positive vibrations don't care how much money you have or what you look like. They are just happy to know you care!

I vibrate with energy because I am energy.

PART 4

SELF-WORTH, LABELS AND HAPPINESS

How much do you value yourself?

•

Labels

•

Happiness is a choice

•

Be happy NOW!

•

Celebrate life

•

Share happiness – SMILE!

How much do you value yourself?

Whether you live in a cardboard box or a mansion, you possess something that someone else would pay their whole life's fortune to have. It could be your health, your eyesight, the love you have in your life, or the knowledge you possess. You see, you already have riches that other people desire, things that money can't buy.

Perceive yourself as a winner and you will win for the rest of your life.

Labels

If you say you're poor, then you have placed a label on yourself. Labels are important. When you see a can of tomatoes on the shelf in the grocery store, you probably have no doubt there are tomatoes inside that can. Why? Because you read the label. So what does *your* label say? If you don't like your present label, change it!

Happiness is a choice

People resist hearing that they can choose happiness. But it's true; you choose your thoughts, which in turn create your experience.

Many people lose sight of how powerful they really are. Yet everyone is born with the power to choose. It can't be taken away!

Why watch the evening news and bombard your mind with violence and sadness? Why not engage the power of happiness instead? It's just as easy to bombard your mind with happy thoughts.

I have a choice
to be happy or unhappy.
I choose happiness.

"Many persons have a wrong idea of what constitutes

true happiness. It is not attained through self gratification,

but through fidelity to a worthy purpose."

— HELEN KELLER

Be happy NOW!

Sometimes it's hard to remain in the present moment. So if you find yourself thinking about the past, think about good times. If your thoughts bring you into the future, visualize happy outcomes.

Make happiness your number one priority now! Don't postpone it. When you are happy, you are more productive to those you love. Share your happiness, and be happy now.

Why be happy?
Because you're worth it!

"To accomplish great things,

you must not only act, but also dream;

not only plan, but also believe."

– ANATOLE FRANCE

Celebrate life

*S*tart by loving yourself NOW. When you love yourself, you will discover a life worth living . . . a life worth celebrating.

Do something that you enjoy every day. At the same time, acknowledge all your gifts and be grateful as you keep discovering the fruits of your journey.

I am a capable human being.
I deserve to love and be loved.

"A happy person is not

a person in a certain set of circumstances,

but rather with a certain set of attitudes."

– HUGH DOWNS

Share happiness – SMILE!

A smile is often greeted with a smile.

A smile is free to give and free to receive.

A smile enriches lives; its memory can last a lifetime.

A smile can bring happiness to the sad and strength to the weak.

Pass on a smile and change a life. It won't cost you a cent.

I will remember to smile at everyone I meet today.

"Don't go backwards, you've already been there."

– RAY CHARLES

PART 5

MOTIVATION, MENTORS AND MANIFESTATION

Motivation

Motivation is fueled by three things: energy, passion, and enthusiasm. To stay in a positive frame of mind, you have to maintain your passion and enthusiasm while directing your energy toward your goals.

Surround yourself with positive motivators—people who praise you and support your accomplishments, symbols, awards, inspiring music or movies like *Rudy*.

Decide what you want to do, then do it!

Dream BIG notes

Sources of inspiration

Write down who and what inspires you here.

Movies:

Songs:

Books:

People:

Other:

Take a mentor to lunch

A mentor is someone who is already living the life you desire. Perhaps this is a person you already know, such as a boss, or maybe it's somebody you don't really know, but have heard or read about.

See if you can get to know them better so you can learn from their wisdom. Contact that person and explain how much he or she has impressed you. Ask your mentor out to lunch—who would say no to a free lunch? This is a great way to get acquainted.

Your potential mentor may not be available the first time you ask. Some people have schedules that are perpetually full. You may have to think of another person to ask. Be persistent; keep going until you find someone willing to mentor you.

Once you have a mentor, always show your appreciation. Offer your assistance in exchange for the knowledge you gain from your mentor's teachings. Make it a win-win situation.

I will find a mentor who will support me and guide me toward my dream.

The key to manifesting desires

Two words hold the key to manifesting your desires: "eliminating doubt."

Doubt kills dreams and finds reasons why something can't be done. Doubt can show up in the form of friends, spouses, or co-workers, and most importantly, your own thoughts. It is important to limit your exposure to all the negative messages from others, and from yourself.

Remember to focus on what you desire. Don't give doubt a second thought! The more doubt you remove, the more you will manifest. Your results will come in proportion to the speed in which you eliminate doubt. The faster you remove doubt, the faster your manifestation.

Give your dream all your attention, energy, and focus.

Dream BIG notes

Purge all those doubts now! Jot down every single dream-busting thought you can think of. Once you've done that, put a line through each of them.

There, you've officially eliminated your doubts!

"Keep away from people who try to belittle your ambitions.

Small people always do that, but the really great make you feel

that you, too, can become great."

– MARK TWAIN

Change your vocabulary

Words have power. The words you choose affect how and what you manifest, and help determine your destiny.

The words you say to yourself are just as important as the words you speak to others. What do you say to yourself and about yourself every day?

Think about the words "I am!" What you place after them carries tremendous impact.

When you change your vocabulary, you change your thoughts, which changes your destiny.

"It's not whether you get knocked down;

it's whether you get up."

— VINCE LOMBARDI

Exercise: "I am _____"

Say the words "I am _____" and then quickly fill in the blank.

Your impulsive first response came from your subconscious. This reaction indicates your knee-jerk impression of yourself and probably reflects how you present yourself to the outside world when you are on "autopilot."

Now do it again, but this time think for a moment.

Now, what is your answer? Chances are it was much more validating. Become more conscious of the way you think of yourself. When you think of yourself as a valued human being, you project your value to others as well.

"The best thing about the future is that

it only comes one day at a time."

— ABRAHAM LINCOLN

Affirtation™ = Affirmation + Quotation

An affirtation is a quotation used with an affirmation to add power to them both. An affirmation is a statement you declare as true. For example, *A journey of a thousand miles starts with one step* is a quotation. Combine it with the affirmation, *I will take that first step toward the thousand-mile journey,* and you have an affirtation.

*Change is a blessing
I am working toward.*

Dream BIG notes

Affirmation + Quotation

Now create some affirtations of your own. Use vocabulary that inspires you. Create at least seven. Repeat them to yourself every day. Choose your strongest affirtations and share them with friends.

1. Quotation:

   Affirmation:

2. Quotation:

   Affirmation:

3. Quotation:

   Affirmation:

4. Quotation:

   Affirmation:

5. Quotation:

   Affirmation:

6. Quotation:

   Affirmation:

7. Quotation:

   Affirmation:

Take care of yourself

Your body is the one and only vessel you have in this life, so take care of it.

Your body is made up of mostly water, so be sure to keep it hydrated.

Feed it clean fuel (that means no processed foods) to ensure optimum performance.

Exercise your mind as well. Stimulate it by reading books, practicing a new language, or learning a musical instrument.

Sleep properly and exercise regularly to alleviate stress.

Relaxation also relieves stress. Meditation is an effective stress-buster.

Exercise: Meditation practice

Take some time each day to meditate in a quiet room. Keep your mind as free from thoughts as possible. If a thought enters your mind, acknowledge it and put it on hold for now. Bask in the feeling of knowing you're taking good care of yourself. It matters.

How can you use meditation to help you commit to manifesting your big dream?

I deserve to relax more and take it easy.

Dream BIG notes

Write down the changes you will make to take better care of yourself.

Eating:

Exercising:

Relaxing:

Become steadfast

Remember, with each passing second, you are either moving closer to or further from your goal. Each day you're given a brand new 24 hours to manifest your dream. So spend your time on actions that will bring you closer to your big dream.

I will be the person I want to be.
I must take action to reach
the things I deserve.

"Somewhere over the rainbow, skies are blue, and the dreams

that you dare to dream really do come true."

— LYMAN FRANK BAUM

Dream BIG notes

What specific actions will take you closer to your dreams?

Keep in mind that persistence develops the strength of your focus. Focus gives you the strength to keep moving toward and attaining your goals. Be persistent and never quit!

Time is perishable

Those who value their time reap more rewards. Make sure other people respect your time as well; don't let them waste it. If someone is always late for appointments, making you wait, let that person know that your time is important.

When you give your time to others, it should be a privilege to them. It's okay to make sure they're aware of that. Having respect for time is crucial because time is perishable. You can never get it back.

"The future depends on what we do in the present."

– MAHATMA GANDHI

PART 6

NOW IS THE TIME
TO TAKE ACTION

What are you willing to trade your time for?

•

Fail forward fast

•

Start to live your dreams

What are you willing to trade your time for?

You traded your time for everything you have in your life. If you lack something, it's because you were unwilling to trade your time for it.

Dream BIG notes

What is the next step you are willing to take *right now* to start manifesting your dreams? No matter how big or small the step, write it down here.

Fail forward fast

Why do most people forget about the dreams they once had? Contributing factors include loss of confidence, lack of self worth, a negative environment, doubt, fear, worry, discouragement—to name a few. Often, it's simply fear of failure.

However, success often results from failure. The trick is to "fail forward" by learning from your mistakes—and learning fast.

Never repeat old mistakes!
Let failure be the mother of success.

"Failure is the opportunity to begin more intelligently."

– HENRY FORD

Start to live your dreams

Remember, life is not a dress rehearsal.

When you dream big and never quit, great things will happen. All it takes is starting.

Declare your dreams now.

It starts with a dream and it's always too soon to quit.

DECLARING MY DREAM

I _____ solemnly declare that
beginning on _____ I will give my dreams all my
attention, energy, and focus.

I know that if it is going to be, it is up to me. I will search out
information, people, and things that will bring me closer to
my dreams.

I will choose to live each day to the fullest, and live in the
moment. I will remain focused, strong, and determined.

I understand I am worth the time and effort it will take to
pursue and achieve my dreams. Under no circumstance will
I allow anyone or anything to pull me away from my dreams.
This declaration is non-negotiable.

SIGN HERE   DATE

"I Can Do This!"

You have sown the seeds of your big dream. You've identified your desires. Now apply the Law of Attraction and ALLOW them into your life.

Let the seeds you planted blossom in full color without a trace of doubt. Nourished by your positive thoughts, your BIG DREAM blooms now.

Much more is REVEALed through our programs and products. Join us today at our website *www.theREVEAL.us*

That's right, just start.
Activate your dreams and live with power!